# Billy Graham

## The Man
## and His Ministry

# Billy Graham

## The Man
## and His Ministry

By Mary Bishop

Grosset & Dunlap

A Filmways Company

Publishers    New York

Designed by Marcia Ben-Eli

Copyright © 1978 by Mary Bishop

Published simultaneously in Canada

Library of Congress catalog card number: 77-87796

ISBN: 0-448-14587-1 (paperback)

ISBN: 0-448-14586-3 (hardcover)

First printing 1978

Printed in the United States

# Contents

# Introduction

There is nobody like him. He has traveled from one country to another for years, giving his counsel to many of the most powerful presidents and heads of state of this century. He has retained the public's affection while dozens of leaders with more official power have fallen by the wayside. This man's name is still a household phrase, and everybody from the diehard cynic to the hero-worshipper is curious about how he really lives and what he really thinks.

Perhaps the most important thing to understand about Billy Graham is that there has never been anything very irregular about him. He is neither too tall nor too short, too intellectual or too folksy; he is neither too harsh nor too subtle in his sin-calling, too Republican or too Democratic in his politics.

He is a celebrity so widely known that nearly anything he says makes news.

While people speculate endlessly about him, Billy Graham steers his life with such caution that it is hard to know whether the private man at all resembles the public one.

Unlike other famous people who sometimes let their hair down—explode with an expletive, an animosity, a frustration, or some normal base desire that gives their observers a glimpse of their emotional life—Billy Graham cannot afford to.

This book admittedly contains many of the old stories, some of them perhaps apocryphal, which have been passed on for years by tellers of the Billy Graham story. It presents much new material also. And it bears some of Graham's thoughts—as revealing in their very phrasing as in their content—gleaned from many hours of interviews with him in 1976.

Billy Graham appears to be headed into a somewhat cloudy future in the late 1970s. He has not in the past volunteered complete financial information on his ministry's wealth. And while there is no indication that his dealings have been anything but legal, there seems to be strong public interest now in total financial disclosure by religious groups. Graham himself has vowed to release public reports henceforth on his organization's financial position. Indeed, how Billy Graham fares in the religious history books may depend on how he emerges from the coming inevitable financial scrutiny.

But woven through the Billy Graham phenomenon is that American awe of success that, unless broken by some traumatic or distracting event or a shift in fashion, will continue to feed a particular success until it has mounted into the near-supernatural. Billy Graham has not gone out of style yet and he may well ride his snowball of success right through retirement.

# 1.
# Country Boyhood

That little Graham boy sure didn't act like preacher material. Sunday mornings, he and his cousins would crawl under the pews in the strict Associate Reformed Presbyterian Church in Charlotte, North Carolina, and propel spitballs with rubber bands at prim women.

His father, a tall, gaunt dairy farmer, would lean over and whisper, "I'll see you when you get home." Once there, he would thrash Billy with his belt.

His parents thought there could be no more desirable future for their elder son than for him to become a minister. Billy Frank Graham, however, thought his own pastor was "sorry" and vowed he'd never be either a preacher or an undertaker. To him, these careers seemed equally dreary.

But Frank and Morrow Coffey Graham did not give up. They sent their son off to three Christian schools after high school, and every night for seven years they prayed he'd become a serious servant of God.

Billy, age six months, being held by his mother, Anne Morrow Coffey Graham.

Their prayers were answered in a grand way: One night in 1944, Catherine Graham, Billy's sister, shrieked, "Oh, Mother, that's Billy Frank!" and the family hovered around a Philco radio to pick up his Chicago sermon over the crackling static.

Her brother's rise from a zestful boy who played Tarzan by trying to swing from trees on his father's farm to a thundering voice of God seemed amazing to Catherine Graham McElroy on another momentous day, this time in 1968. Her sister Jean, brother Melvin, and their mother were standing in a doorway at their family home in Charlotte, waiting for Richard Nixon.

Thirty-five years before, Catherine remembered, she had been standing in the same doorway, gulping chocolate milk and waiting for the school bus. "Who would ever have thought a farm family like this would be waiting for the [former] Vice President?" she said as she watched Nixon's car approach the house.

Charlotte, North Carolina, was a natural spawning ground for a conservative, hard-working prudent evangelist like Billy Graham, and the Graham home nurtured a strong masculine figure who would be admired by powerful men.

Billy Graham's upbringing wasn't so rigid as to make him rebel against it, but discipline and fear of God turned him into a well-behaved young man, a respecter of authority, the model "good citizen" he became for so many people.

Piety evolved slowly in the Graham family, however.

His paternal grandfather, Crook Graham, was a cursing Confederate veteran who drank corn whisky he got illegally from a drugstore, much to the dismay of his more orthodox wife. Crook would sometimes sit drunk at the organ in his home, singing and weeping.

Crook's son Frank Graham was a much more righteous sort. He was a regular at church and a school board member, though his younger son Melvin says that he could barely read or write. Regular at his work, also, he labored like the mule he thought was the farmer's best helper.

God, work and self-discipline were supreme in the Graham home. Billy's mother walked a quarter-mile to pick beans the day before his birth November 7, 1918. Her Bible accompanied her everywhere, even on her honeymoon, and she and her late husband had daily family devotions. Their children read Bible verses before school, and by the time he was ten Billy had learned answers to the 107 questions of the Shorter Catechism—from "What is the chief end of man?" to "What doth the conclusion of the Lord's prayer teach us?"

"I had been raised in a very strict Presbyterian home," said his mother, "and that's what I wanted for my children." She used to polish her shoes and do all other weekend chores on Saturdays as a child so she could keep the Sabbath untainted by work.

One of her favorite Bible passages is still Deuteronomy 6:5–7—"And thou shalt love the Lord thy God with all thine heart, and with all thy soul, and with all thy might. And these words, which I command thee this day, shall be in thine heart. And thou shalt teach them diligently unto thy children, and shalt talk of them when thou sittest in thine house."

Frank Graham would often wake Billy Frank at 2:30 A.M. to milk some of the family's twenty-seven cows before school. When boys gathered at the Graham's to play football after school, Billy couldn't join them until he'd finished his chores. But his father indulged Billy in other ways. He bought him all the Tarzan books, and Billy also read the Rover Boys and Tom Swift series.

Between morning farm work and baseball practice, which sometimes lasted until midnight, Billy was a drowsy and undistinguished student.

Connor R. Hutchison, principal and teacher at Sharon School in Charlotte when Graham was there, said, "Billy always sat right near my teacher's desk and he was very conscientious, but one of my problems was keeping him awake."

Graham himself says: "I didn't do well in high school at all, did very poorly, I think. . . . In those days if you were on a [sports] team, that's about all you had to do at high school. . . . Some of the teachers didn't really hold your nose to the grindstone."

Young Billy sometimes was a daring prankster—in sharp contrast to his life today as a walking evangelistic institution who must watch his every word and action.

In the eighth grade, according to his boyhood buddy Winston Covington, "We had a general science teacher and she let us get away with murder. The thing that really straightened us out was when we emptied a trash basket, set it on fire, yelled 'Fire!' and jumped out the window of the one-story school."

Graham said he "regrets to say" the story is true. There was no serious damage but his parents were furious.

Not all his teachers foresaw great things in the skinny Graham kid. Covington said that one day in senior year when Graham was absent, a teacher announced to the class that Billy "would never amount to anything."

Covington, now a Charlotte telephone company executive, recalls their high school days when he and Graham "would drive around and hug and kiss our dates and find a lonely spot. He was in love and out of love almost weekly. He liked to dress nice, liked new, nice automobiles and girls. I guess financially he and I had as much as anybody in school."

During the Depression, the Graham children shared with their poorer friends the penny candy and ice cream cones they bought Fridays with their nickel allowance. Their friends thought they were rich, said Catherine Graham McElroy.

# 2.
# Spiritual Odyssey

In the fall of 1934, when he was sixteen, Billy Frank Graham began a spiritual odyssey. He started by shaking a moral finger at the cussing and indiscretions (from Billy's point of view) of his classmates and wound up years later preaching to the whole world.

The moral climate that fall was an ideal catalyst for Billy Graham's new piety—several workers were killed at Carolina cotton mills during a national strike; police arrested Bruno Hauptmann in the kidnaping and murder of Charles Lindbergh's baby son; police combed the country for John Dillinger. Like F. Scott Fitzgerald's *Tender Is the Night*, the haunting 1934 novel about Americans on the moral skids, the news that fall suggested that people were losing their grip.

Some Christians hurled down iron-handed judgments. People who went to movies on Sunday in Charlotte were called satanic. Temperance activists bemoaned the city's first year of legal beer sales.

Frank Graham and other Christian men asked Kentucky fire-and-brimstoner Mordecai Fowler Ham to hold a revival in Charlotte.

In a raw pine tabernacle where a paint store is now, Ham railed against card-playing and movies ("I cannot take joy in the movies because I know what is behind the screen.") He told Charlotte that its "Anglo-Saxon background makes it the finest field for Christian work." He fired away at local pastors and enraged Charlotte's mayor by charging that high school students there were "patronizing houses of ill fame." He never substantiated the charge.

The Rev. Grady Wilson, a longtime friend of Graham's and one of his associate evangelists, said that before he died, a weeping Ham told him: "I used to go into a city for a citywide crusade and I would skin the ministers from snout to tail. . . . I'd tack their hide on the wall and then I'd rub the salt in. . . . Great crowds would come and I became a controversial evangelist. I'm sorry about the whole bit."

Graham now says he frowns on such abrasive evangelism, but one night in the fall of 1934, he and Grady Wilson, then fifteen, were swept up in Ham's harvest of "saved" souls.

Billy Frank had been to other meetings in the Ham crusade. One time he had hidden behind the hat of a woman in front of him as the evangelist pointed his way and roared "You're a sinner!" On the night that all that finger-pointing really got results, the crowd had just sung "When the Roll Is Called Up Yonder" and Ham launched into a sermon with the stern announcement "There's a great sinner in this place tonight." Billy Frank Graham wondered if his mother had told the evangelist about him, according to an old Graham family friend's account of young Billy's decision for Christ.

The choir sang "Just As I Am, Without One Plea"— the same old hymn Graham uses to bring the faithful down the aisles of coliseums today—and Billy and Grady were urged to heed Ham's call to salvation by a

(WORLD WIDE)

Charlotte men's clothier. Little did the two young men know, as they walked the sawdust trail that night, that they would spend twenty-nine years together making that appeal around the world.

The next day at school, Graham relates, "One of my teachers said to me with a sneer, 'Preacher Graham, I hear you got religion last night.' . . . That was my persecution."

But Billy was popular, girls thought him handsome, and, besides, "getting religion" wasn't so out of vogue then, especially not in Bible Belt Charlotte.

After Billy's conversion, he gave Winston Covington a hard time for the cursing he'd picked up from a farmhand and teased him for taking college geology, calling its physical history of the earth "too scientific" for a real Christian. Covington says Billy wouldn't take a drink "and certainly never took the Lord's name in vain."

Billy's graduation picture from Sharon High School in Charlotte, North Carolina.

(WORLD WIDE)

**Photograph taken of Billy at about the age of 19 in one of the fields near his home in Charlotte, North Carolina.**

Pauline Shanks, now a Charlotte grandmother, dated Graham when he was in high school. "I do not remember him ever using even slang," she says. "The most he'd say was 'good gracious' or something. He was tall with real blond hair and blue eyes—real good-looking. Billy was the sort of person that you really liked. He was a great date."

Graham, like his father, was not a dancer. Frank Graham had been "saved" the night after he had been out dancing when he was eighteen, and when Billy went to his first high school party after his own conversion, his mother related, he vowed to come straight home if there was any dancing. "Sure enough," she said, "about ten o'clock he came in."

The summer after his high school graduation in 1936, Graham, Grady Wilson and his brother, T. W. Wilson, sold Fuller brushes door-to-door in the Carolinas. "There was no doubt about it—Billy was the supersalesman," says the Rev. T. W. Wilson, now Graham's aide-de-camp. When the Wilson boys took swimming breaks, Billy kept selling brushes.

Even then Graham exuded the conviction he uses today to market the word of God. He convinced housewife after housewife she desperately needed a Fuller brush. According to the authorized 1966 biography by John Pollock, Graham prayed before each house call.

Graham and the Wilson brothers were beginning to venture beyond Charlotte and sometimes encountered unpleasantries absent in their comfortable homes. They stayed at a cheap hotel in the little North Carolina town of Monroe while attending a revival and were awakened in the night by bed bugs. The rest of the night they slept on shavings covering the floor of the revival tabernacle.

Graham had wanted to go to the University of North Carolina, but his mother chose ultraconservative, fundamentalist Bob Jones College in Cleveland, Tennessee (now Bob Jones University in Greenville, South Carolina). But the sternness there was too much even for Billy, and he quit after a semester.

His mother, still insisting he get a "Christian" education, sent him to Florida Bible Institute at Temple Terrace near Tampa, Florida, now Trinity College in Dunedin, Florida. He liked the sun, the less authoritarian Bible study and the exposure to vacationing big-name evangelicals. And the new school allowed dating, which Bob Jones had restricted.

Back in Charlotte, Frank and Morrow Graham were praying in their bedroom every night that Billy would follow the Apostle Paul's instruction to young Timothy: "Study to shew thyself approved unto God, a workman that needeth not to be ashamed, rightly dividing the word of truth."

## An Eighteenth-Hole Surrender

(WORLD WIDE)

Friends at the Institute were telling Billy that God was calling him to preach, but Graham wasn't sure he wanted to heed the call. "I always hated the ministry," Graham later recalled.

But one night in March, 1938, on the Institute's golf course, Graham had his famous, tearful eighteenth-hole surrender to God.

"I was struggling with the call to preach . . . ," he said later. "There was an inner voice that said, 'You must preach, you must preach.' I said, 'Yes, Lord, if you want me, I'll preach.'"

Later, when Graham was student-preaching the gospel in Tampa trailer parks, he was still not confident of his sermon style. He practiced alone in the swamps and in an old garage where students would sneak up and yell, "Amen!"

Dr. W. T. Watson, president of Florida Bible Institute when Graham was there, recalls, "He'd get out and preach to a stump, anything that would stand still."

In his second year at the Institute, the 6-foot-2½-

inch Graham, with his flashing smile, blue eyes and thick, wavy blond hair, fell in love with fellow student Emily Cavanaugh. They became engaged.

In one of the most-chronicled heartbreaks of Graham's life, she broke with him and married Charles Massey, another Institute student and a friend of Graham. Massey became a colonel in the Army chaplaincy and is now a professor at Trinity College.

"One story said that she said that I was never going to amount to anything and Charlie was," Graham said. "Well, that wasn't quite it. . . . I think she probably *thought* that, because I didn't have any goal in life at all, even though we were engaged to be married. I was studying the Bible but wasn't terribly interested, and she and this other fella—he knew where he was going."

The Masseys are weary of the jilting story and Col. Massey does not like his wife to be asked about it. Mrs. Massey said her breakup with Graham was "very traumatic. He was more serious than I. I felt that in fairness to him I should break it off. In college, neither of our characters were fully formed . . . but I never said anything derogatory to him or anybody else."

The experience embarrassed Graham at least a little: "I went to their wedding and . . . they sat me with her family and everybody in the church knew. . . . That experience was a turning point in my life because it really got me down to the business of God, and from that point I said, 'Lord, I'm only going to marry the person of your choice.' So I forgot girls for a long time, two or three years."

Graham earned the Institute's Christian Worker's diploma; in those days degrees were not granted. His mother and prominent evangelicals who met Graham in Florida urged him to get a degree from Wheaton College in Wheaton, Illinois, one of the nation's best-known evangelical colleges.

At Wheaton, Graham majored in anthropology. "I suppose God was preparing me for my world minis-

(WORLD WIDE)

Back in his student days at the Florida Bible Institute, Billy poses with Dean Minder.

try," Graham says, "because it taught me customs, culture and so forth of peoples on every continent."

At Wheaton, he met Ruth Bell, a graceful, fine-boned, aristocratic-looking young woman majoring in Bible and working hard to become, like her parents, a Presbyterian missionary to China.

"The moment I met her," says Graham, "I knew she was the one. . . . When I first met her, she was a junior at Wheaton and I was a freshman and I drove a furniture truck lifting furniture. This fella that owned the business kept telling me about this wonderful girl from China and he had built her up to such a point that I was in great expectancy before I met her and when he introduced me to her I was already pretty well decided that's the girl for me."

## Mountain Honeymoon

Ruth Bell scrapped her missionary plans for Billy. She says he told her, "It's your business to follow and the Lord will lead me." They were married after their graduation from Wheaton in 1943. Graham was twenty-four and Ruth twenty-three.

After a honeymoon in a two-dollars-a-night room at Blowing Rock, in the North Carolina mountains, Graham returned to his new job as pastor of a little Baptist church in Western Springs, Illinois. The pay: forty-five dollars a week.

That year, a Chicago radio evangelist spotted Graham's robust preaching and put him on *Songs in the Night,* a live weekly radio preaching broadcast, the show that brought Graham's family excitedly together around their Philco radio to hear him preaching so far away.

Then Graham led evangelistic rallies around the country for Youth for Christ, a fundamentalist group. He wore loud, hand-painted ties and garish suits, and the Youth for Christ team used gimmicks, including 100 pianos playing together, to dazzle young people.

But in 1948, Graham was off and running on his

own, first with a church-supported crusade in Augusta, Georgia. A year later, his Los Angeles crusade enthralled newspaper magnate William Randolph Hearst, who told his papers to "puff Graham." The evangelist, just thirty, was on his way to becoming the hottest revivalist since Billy Sunday, who had been leading massive campaigns for Christ when Graham was born.

At a time when Graham's fame was growing around the world, he feared he was becoming a stranger in his own home. He recalls one night when he returned from a long trip and found his toddler son, Franklin, sleeping in his mother's room. The boy awoke and asked his mother, "Who him?"

A sad moment for Graham was recounted by his eldest daughter, Virginia, called Gigi. When she was a little girl, she told biographer John Pollock, "I had been very rude, and he spanked me. I asked him in anger what kind of father he thought he was anyway, always being gone. Tears filled his eyes. . . . Now, as a parent, I understand quite fully the anguish he must have gone through at times, wondering if he was making the right decision by leaving."

With her husband away for months at time, Ruth Graham settled their growing family with her parents in the Buncombe County village of Montreat in the North Carolina mountains. Her father, Dr. L. Nelson Bell, had become a surgeon in nearby Asheville and a leading Presbyterian conservative after Chinese communists expelled him and other missionaries from the country.

A caretaker for the Grahams filled some parental functions for the children, Gigi, Anne, Bunny, Franklin and Ned.

"He [the caretaker] taught me hunting and things a father would teach a son, and I had a pastor who took me fishing," recalls Franklin, who now has two children of his own.

Once a rebellious teenager, Franklin says he "was

(WORLD WIDE)

kind of a hard-headed individual. I smoked and I drank beer, not bad things.'' He wants to go into full-time Christian work now but doubts he'll be an evangelist. ''. . . I think I might make a fool out of Christ's name and maybe my father's name,'' he explains.

In spite of his long absences, Billy Graham always exerted a strong influence on his home. That tradition was also his parents'. His mother never learned to drive, she says, because her husband thought it was ''the man's place to drive.''

Billy Graham's wife and mother abide by what they see as the imperative of Ephesians 5:22–24: ''Wives, submit yourselves unto your own husbands, as unto the Lord. For the husband is the head of the wife, even as Christ is the head of the Church . . .''

While Graham will voice approval for some aims of the women's movement, such as the ordination of women in the clergy, he thinks the changes in sex roles can threaten the Bible's prescription for a Christian home. ''The so-called emancipation of women,'' he says, ''causes young women to postpone marriage and older women to get out of it as soon as they can.'' The women's movement, he says, is ''freeing the man from his responsibilities as head of the home.''

''When a woman gets married today,'' Graham says, ''she has very little security that the marriage will last unless it's a marriage in Christ.''

Ruth Graham told students at a college in Seattle in 1976 that Graham ''hasn't heard of women's lib.'' She said she had followed her husband's wishes that particular day by changing from a pants suit to a dress for her speech on the Christian campus, where bus stop graffiti said ''Jesus loves even me.''

''I told her I thought it would be much more proper if she wore a dress before a student body and a faculty,'' Graham said later.

Ruth Graham is a halting, nervous speaker, but Graham and his assistants say they respect her intelli-

(WIDE WORLD PHOTO)

**Billy and Ruth Graham leaving St. Giles' Cathedral, Edinburgh, Scotland.**

(WIDE WORLD PHOTO)

Above: Ruth and Billy with his dairy farmer dad.

Left: Billy Graham with his parents, William Franklin, Sr. and Anne Morrow Graham, at the Columbia, South Carolina Crusade, 1950.

Below: Aboard the HAWAI-IAN RANCHER the evange-list and his wife sail for some marlin fishing at Kona, Hawaii.

(THE CHARLOTTE OBSERVER)

Billy and Ruth at a surprise 40th birthday party given him by his staff.

(WIDE WORLD PHOTO)

15

gence and knowledge of the scripture. "She's a real student of the Bible, far more than I am," Graham says.

His wife freely tugs at Graham's conscience and teases him.

She doesn't know why God "chose" him to be such a spiritual force, she says. "Maybe it's because he doesn't have all that many natural talents," is one of her standard joking lines.

It was Ruth Graham, says the evangelist, who warned him not to dabble in political matters but to keep his advice "spiritual"—advice Graham now says he should have taken.

Graham gets annoyed at being called a jet setter. "Ninety per cent of my time," he says, "is spent with just ordinary, common people. If I play golf with Arnold Palmer, that's news. If I play golf with Joe Blow, which is ninety per cent of the time . . . that's not news."

The country boy from Charlotte also talks of his concern for simple folk, yet he doesn't like to be thought of as a backwoods fundamentalist.

The Grahams moved to their big log cabin in the early 1950s from a gray stone house down the mountain. One reason they moved was to get away from the tourists who pressed their noses against the windows to watch the Grahams eat.

Graham's life has been threatened in almost every American city where he has held a crusade, according to his aide T. W. Wilson, who often registers for the evangelist at hotels, answers his door and stays close during crusades.

Graham has told his wife and colleagues not to pay ransom if he should ever be kidnaped. "When God's time comes for us, that's God's time," he says. Mrs. Graham says she doesn't worry: "Nothing could touch a child of God without His permission."

Yet two part-time security guards have watched over Graham at Montreat, and local plainclothes

(THE CHARLOTTE OBSERVER)

**Posing with 'Friend' on his father's farm.**

policemen have guarded him at crusades.

With T. W. Wilson and other Graham co-workers and protectors surrounding him at crusades, Mrs. Graham doesn't get much time alone with him and often stays home. "It's like a general taking his wife to battle," she says of her trips to crusades.

But the Grahams and the evangelist's right-hand people profess great love for each other. There's an old story about Mrs. Graham once being so worried about Grady Wilson taking some yellow sleeping capsules that she emptied them and refilled them with mustard powder.

**En route to Australia for an extensive tour, Billy and Ruth Graham enjoy a brief respite in the Hawaiian Islands.**

# 3.
# About the House

The Graham house is quieter now that the children are grown and on their own.

Gigi lives in Milwaukee with her husband, psychologist Stephan Tchividjian, and their five children. Anne is married to former University of North Carolina basketball star Danny Lotz, who is now a Raleigh, North Carolina dentist, and they have three children. Bunny, of Philadelphia, and her husband, Ted Dienert, an executive for an advertising firm that does Graham's work, have two children. Franklin and his wife, the former Jean Cunningham, have two sons, including little William Franklin Graham IV. And the Graham's youngest, Ned, has just been graduated from a private high school on Long Island.

When Graham is home, he says, he gets up at 7:30 to watch the NBC *Today* show or the CBS *Morning News*. He's quick to point out that he can't pick up an ABC station on his mountaintop so he can't see *Good Morning, America*.

He usually eats a big breakfast, often including grapefruit, an egg, bran flakes, grits, and two cups of coffee. He and Mrs. Graham and perhaps Beatrice Long, their housekeeper for more than twenty years, have devotions—a scriptural passage of about six verses and a prayer.

The evangelist often spends most of the day at home working on new books, and he's pumping them out one a year these days. Graham is keenly attuned to public interests. The title of his latest book *How To Be Born Again* was changed from *How To Be Saved,* he said, because of the interest prompted by Jimmy Carter's use of the words "born again."

Graham says he also studies theology and skims such publications as the *Religious News Service*, the *Evangelical News Service*, the *Catholic News Service*, the *Sword of the Lord, Christian Science Monitor*, the *Charlotte Observer*, the *New York Times*, the *Washington Post*, the *London Daily Express*, the *London Daily Telegraph* and the *Guardian*.

He likes the British papers, he says, because he thinks their political writers have a better "knowledge of the facts" than American ones and points to British journalists' recent warnings about communism, Russia, and Britain's "lack of defense" as examples of their political acumen.

When Graham wanders into the pantry for a snack, he is likely to open a can of Vienna sausages, baked beans or sardines, but he avoids salt because of his high blood pressure—about 135/90 if he doesn't take medication for it. He likes to keep his weight at 172. Until a bout with thrombo-phlebitis early in 1976, Graham jogged a mile and a half a day or treaded water in a five-foot-deep bathtub.

Graham has almost given up golf because it's too time-consuming and expensive, he says, and because golf carts offer little exercise. He belongs to four golf clubs. He pays for memberships in the Black Mountain Country Club at home and the Biltmore Country Club

**After a round of golf on the King's Golf Course at Gleneagles, Scotland.**

**Right: Mrs. Frank Graham serves her son a favorite dish.**

in nearby Asheville. Hugh Morton, developer of the Grandfather Mountain resort in North Carolina, pays for Graham's membership at Grandfather Mountain Country Club. Jack Nicklaus, the golfer, gave him a membership at Johns Island Country Club in Vero Beach, Florida.

Graham works to keep his powerful voice in shape, too. When he and T. W. Wilson are driving alone, Graham lubricates his vocal cords by booming "YES! YES! YES! NO! NO! NO!" Wilson jokingly threatens to sue Graham for deafening him.

Billy Graham also exercises his eyes by rolling them. He told a group of ministers and lay people at one of his Billy Graham Schools of Evangelism in 1976 that

**Left: The family (from left): Ned, Bunny and Ted Dienert, Stephan and Gigi Tchivodjain with their children, the Grahams, Ann and Danny Lotz with their children, and Franklin Graham.**

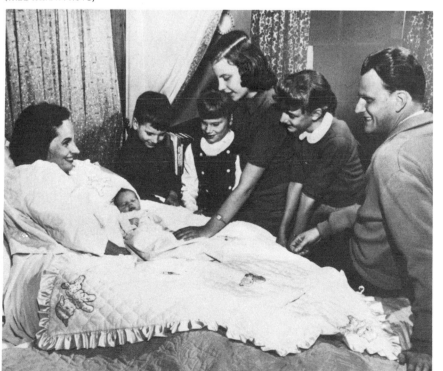

**Above: Reunion aboard the liner QUEEN ELIZABETH: Graham holds Ned, 2. Other children, from left, are: Anne, 12; Gigi, 15; Franklin, 8; and Bunny, 9.**

**Left: The family gathers to admire the latest addition, Nelson Edmund, born January 17, 1958.**

(WIDE WORLD PHOTO)

**Right: Billy Graham sits in the doorway of the 10-room log and timber house that sits atop a mountain.**

**Ruth Graham is met by her husband at the Los Angeles International Airport as she arrives for the closing meeting of the Southern California Crusade in September, 1963.**

(WIDE WORLD PHOTO)

the American Bible Society gave him a large-print Bible to use in the pulpit. But, he told them, "It's getting close to where the type will have to be larger, or I'll have to wear glasses on television." (A minister in the audience whispered to nobody in particular, "Is that his Achilles heel?") Graham expects to be wearing glasses or contact lenses on television within the next two years.

He's on display much of the time, but at Montreat the local folks are protective of the Grahams and try to keep tourists from hassling them. A retired minister there used to like to play dumb to pesky Graham-hunting tourists who would approach him as he worked in his yard. "Billy who?" the old fellow would ask. "You know, Billy *Graham*," the travelers would plead, astonished at his ignorance. But the cleric wouldn't budge. He'd say, "I'm sorry, I don't know who you mean" and keep on working.

Uva Miracle, news editor of the weekly *Black Mountain News* and longtime friend of the Grahams, said, "If Billy is in a restaurant eating, we just nod and go on. We treat 'em like folks. We try to leave them alone.

If Ruth is in the grocery store shopping, we don't let on that Ruth is in the grocery store shopping."

Outside Montreat, Billy Graham can travel unbothered only in countries where his crusades aren't televised, but there aren't many since he's been on television in about forty-eight countries.

He doesn't own a home abroad. "I have enough friends who invite me to come stay with them all over the world, that I don't have to worry about [foreign] property."

Billy Graham insists there's nothing intoxicating about being Billy Graham. "It was always very humbling and frightening," he says. "I was frightened I would do something that would bring disrepute to Christ, to the kingdom of God. I wasn't prepared for it. I had to learn it fast. I had to study hard and discipline myself. There's nothing heady about it. If I'd gotten heady, the Lord would have kicked me down, which he does periodically."

After spreading the gospel almost nonstop for more than thirty years, Graham expects to retire in the early 1980s. He often seems weary. "My greatest longing," he says, "is for privacy."

**Billy Graham addresses an overflow crowd from the steps of the Lincoln Memorial on Honor America Day (1970).**

# 4.

# The Preacher

There are two ways to explain why Billy Graham became the best-known evangelist in the world.

First, he has the power of God behind him. That's the primary reason Graham gives for his success.

Second, he has been endowed with everything an evangelist needs for a broad appeal:

> He is a compelling physical figure, with his majestic Charlton Heston handsomeness and his mighty voice. As people who tried for years to get him to run for public office know, Graham inspires confidence.

> He has a sophisticated organization that pioneered in adapting evangelism to television and other media. When other evangelists were getting bad press, Graham had early support from two of the nation's most prominent press giants, William Randolph Hearst and Henry Luce.

His theology doesn't demand economic self-denial, doesn't turn off the rich, the powerful, the conservative and the patriotic, and doesn't confuse people of a simple faith. In glowing terms, he offers forgiveness and everlasting life to people haunted by guilt and afraid of damnation.

Graham inherited more than 200 years of experimentation by American evangelists—George Whitefield's infectious eighteenth-century preaching that made even the grimmest, most fatalistic Calvinists believe they might have a chance at heaven; Charles Grandison Finney's nineteenth-century practice of having people come forward to the "anxious seat" to be saved at the end of mass meetings; Dwight L. Moody's heavy emphasis on the Bible in the late nineteen century; and farmboy Billy Sunday's efficient crusades and backing by wealthy buddies like George Armour and Cyrus McCormick sixty years ago.

"I'm not a great preacher as analyzed by clergy or professors in seminaries," Graham says, "and if you read the sermons that evangelists have preached down through the centuries, I think you'll find the same thing."

There are many fundamentalist evangelists today—those who share Graham's belief in the authority and divine inspiration of the Bible, the virgin birth of Christ, Christ's washing away of our sins on the cross, the bodily resurrection of Jesus and His second coming.

And Graham is not the first big crowd raiser for evangelism. In his sixteen-week 1957 crusade in New York City, he drew 2,397,000 people. Billy Sunday attracted 1,443,000 in his ten-week campaign there in 1917—only about 5,500 fewer people a week than Graham.

But Billy Graham personifies evangelism to a far greater extent than his predecessors and contemporaries, religious historians say, because he and television were born as public phenomena at about the

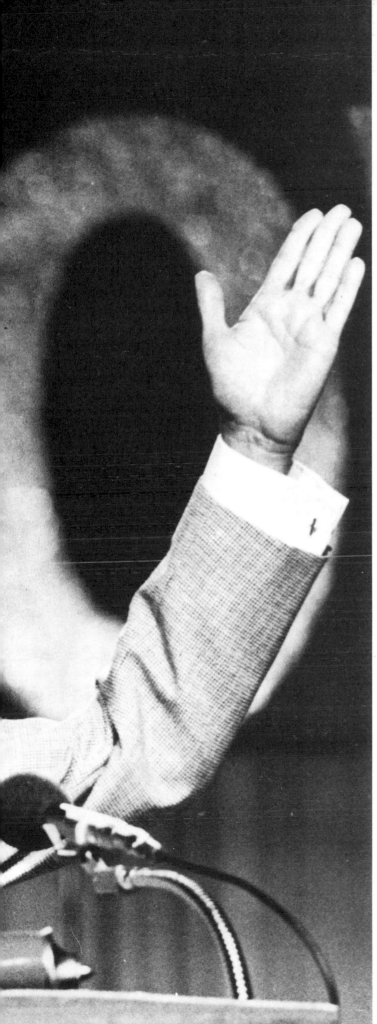

**Above:**
**Mingling with the young people at a rock concert in Hollywood, California.**

31

same time—the late 1940s—and because he has used all the media so well.

American religious history shows that at the end of World War II, for the first time in many years, the demand for evangelists outstripped the supply.

In an electronic age that has crowded our heads with familiar faces and names and instant word associations, Billy Graham has become as synonymous with evangelism as Campbell's is with soup.

His Billy Graham Evangelistic Association, with a staff of 478, and his other organizations spent millions of dollars in 1976 spreading God's word through the works of Billy Graham. These organizations make up a veritable corps of Christian soldiers, and Graham sometimes sounds like its four-star general. "As long as there's a soul to be won to Christ," he says, "I'm under orders by the Lord to go try to win that soul to Christ."

In about 150 crusades since 1947, Graham has preached in person to an estimated eighty million people.

He has written twelve books and given away more than forty-eight million copies of his sermons. His studio has produced more than 100 films. And more than 900 radio stations carry his weekly program.

## The Lord, Not Marketing

But he and his aides say it's mainly the Lord—not clever marketing—that has made him a success.

Seattle's Kingdome was packed with 74,000 people and 15,000 more were turned away the night Johnny Cash appeared at a Graham crusade in May, 1976. Graham claimed it was the biggest indoor gathering in Pacific Northwest history. But he gave credit to the Lord, not to Cash, as the drawing card.

Former British Prime Minister Winston Churchill once told Graham that if he had had actress Marilyn Monroe and other celebrities perform free in London he couldn't have drawn bigger crowds than Graham did in a 1954 crusade.

One key to Graham's success is his organization's recruiting of thousands of volunteers. Says Sterling Huston, crusade director of the Billy Graham Evangelistic Association and a former industrial engineer for Eastman Kodak:

"You get a guy working as an usher and he brings his whole family. . . . You get a guy hammering nails and his family comes to see what's going on. We try to involve the maximum number of people because their involvement is a commitment to be there."

After his organizers had recruited thousands of ushers, choir members and counselors for the Seattle crusade and it was a roaring success, Graham said, "The preparation has been so tremendous, you could stand up there every night and give John 3:16 ('For God so loved the world, that He gave His only begotten Son . . .') and the people would come."

In spite of all that organization, Jean Graham Ford, Billy Graham's younger sister, said of her brother's success, "There's no way to humanly explain it, except that it was in the providence of God."

"There's something else, you see," Graham tells analyzers of his crusade planning. "There is the power of the spirit of God."

There also has been the power of the news media.

William Randolph Hearst told his newspaper chain in 1949 to "Puff Graham." Henry Luce, founder of *Time* and *Life* magazines, went to Columbia, South Carolina, in 1950 to see a crusade by Graham, then just thirty-one, and dispatched a *Life* team there for a story.

According to John Pollock's 1966 authorized biography of Graham, the evangelist complained to Luce that *Time* had sent "a secularist, ignorant and suspicious of the concept and message of evangelism" to cover his Los Angeles crusade in 1949. "Would you send a dress designer to cover a ball game?" Graham reportedly asked Luce. The biography continues, "Luce took the point. *Time* and *Life* eventually became eminently fair and objective."

"He [Luce] and I became very close friends," says Graham. *"Time* . . . pushed me all the time by carrying everything I did, almost. That gave universities and colleges a serious look at me that they would not normally have taken, had it not been written up in a sophisticated publication like *Time."*

From those early boosts, Billy Graham went on to become more than just a man. He became a commodity, the trademark of an enormous enterprise, and sometimes he belies his awareness of himself as an institution in the use of pronouns. For instance, he said in 1976, "You know, I had so much coverage in the fifties. If you went through the scrapbooks you wouldn't believe it because we received the award two years straight as being most publicized person in the United States, including President Eisenhower. More copy was carried on me than the President.

"Let's see, I was on the front cover of *Look* at least seven or eight times, on the front cover of *Newsweek* seven or eight times, on the front cover of *Time* only once, on the front cover of *Life* four times."

Graham still has admirers among prominent journalists.

One, George Cornell, religion writer for the Associated Press, went forward to recommit his life to Christ at Graham's 1957 New York crusade while fellow reporters were making "the usual sardonic comments" about the evangelist. He considers Graham "a good friend" and "a charming, likable guy."

## Softer Hallelujahs

When Graham started out, he had to fight the Elmer Gantry stereotype of the wild-eyed, greedy manipulator of people's emotions.

Early on, Graham stopped denouncing "commies"

(WIDE WORLD PHOTO)

(THE CHARLOTTE OBSERVER)

and "pinks" and shed his white spats and pulpit acrobatics. Music director Cliff Barrows put his trombone away, and the crusade team toned down what Grady Wilson calls "the loud hallelujahs."

Graham doesn't like to be called a "fundamentalist" because he thinks the word connotes ignorance, financial irresponsibility, snake handling and an obsession with hell. He says he's more interested in the love of God.

Still, he continues to jump on the excesses of sex, drinking, drugs, gambling and smoking. But his language is more palatable than, say, Billy Sunday's, who lambasted the "hog-jowled, weasel-eyed, sponge-columned, mushy-fisted, jelly-spined, pussy-footing, four-flushing, Charlotte-russe Christians."

A master of evangelistic diplomacy, Billy Graham usually does not attack specific groups. His is evangelism in good taste.

Billy Graham, who considers himself an ambassador for God, uses the tact of an emissary in the pulpit. He steps on sinner's toes *gently*. Because Graham mixes a paternal concern with his moral chiding, few people are liable to come away from a Graham sermon muttering, "Who does he think *he* is?"

But when Billy Graham stands at his crusade pulpit, custom-made for him by IBM with a built-in clock and lights that warn him when there are five, three and one minute of preaching time left, he is, like his evangelistic forebears, out to scare the hell—fate of unrepentant sinners—out of his hearers. He wants to replace that future with what one of his singers calls "mansions in heaven."

There is a romantic air to the crusades. Women like Evie Tornquist, an angel-faced young blonde of Scandinavian origin, sing love songs to Christ. "I surrender all," she croons, waving an imaginary white flag to dramatize her submission to the Lord.

The sheer size of the crusade crown makes it a religious experience. "You can't walk into a coliseum and hear a thousand people singing without the hairs on the back of your neck standing up,'' says the Rev. James Johnson, a Charlotte pastor turned counselor who worked on Graham crusades.

Young children can get the message at a Graham crusade. Years ago, Graham took the advice of his friend, the late vocabulary buff J. Howard Pew, president of Sun Oil Company, to stop using big words in sermons.

Graham looks venerable, like an old eagle, with his silver sideburns, his sharp nose and his gaze made more formidable by the deep frown wrinkles between his frosty eyebrows. For those who respond with awe to strong male body language, Graham is a magnificent specimen, a Valentino for the Lord.

The jaw is firm and snaps shut in teeth-grinding seriousness after a biting remark. The face is stern, almost angry. There are no gestures of equivocation, no apologetic mannerisms. The head doesn't tilt in a pleading gesture. There is no squinting, no shoulder-shrugging, no lip-puckering, no sweet talk.

His urgings are more commands than pleadings, and his forceful gestures are an effective accompaniment. His index finger chops the air, jabs at his audience. His fists thrust forward.

"It will someday be too late for your soul,'' he booms. "It may be too late for some of you tonight. . . . Don't let this moment pass because it may never come again.''

"God is speaking to you tonight,'' he says, hypnotically. "There's a little voice that says you should come. You're resisting.''

Billy Graham must have a diaphragm of steel. With the force and clarity of a veteran King Lear, he "Pro-o-o-JECTS!'' his voice, as his aide T. W. Wilson says, to the last row of the uppermost tier of a coliseum.

## High Drama for the Lord

After all these years, Graham says it's easier for him

(WIDE WORLD PHOTO)

**Enjoying an ice cream soda with a group of teen-agers after discussing the problem of juvenile crime at a New York City news conference.**

to talk to big crowds than to individuals. But he sometimes gives private counsel. An American Airlines pilot plopped down beside him on a flight a few years ago and got two hours of guidance from the world's best-known evangelist.

In the pulpit, Graham's performance is high drama for the Lord. The sounds alone are entertaining, varied, never dull. Some syllables are staccato, others curl up, dance around, until he reaches a higher pitch for a lofty spiritual appeal. Then—whomp!—the hearer is left hanging for a moment of silence and Graham is back to a story-telling, living-room tone for a personal story.

There's a trace of the aristocratic South in his voice. "Honolulu" is "Honolulah." "Remember" is "Remembah," and "dollar" is "dollah."

As a choir of thousands softly sing "Just As I Am, Without One Plea," Graham beckons the masses to surrender their lives to Christ. And they come—old men clutching balled-up handkerchiefs, teen-age women giggling self-consciously together, couples holding hands, and hundreds of people marching forward as unemotionally as if they were crossing the street to pick up a quart of milk rather than laying claim to eternal life.

When they gather at Graham's feet, he usually has his right hand to his chin and looks off in the distance.

"I'm looking primarily at the people coming forward," he says. "Many times I look right down into their eyes. In fact, I try to look at each one for just a split second if I possibly can so as to give them a little sense of personal relationship and the fact that I'm happy that they're making this commitment.

"I feel terribly unworthy at that moment. I feel terribly inadequate to help them. I know it has to be of God, that I can't do anything, that they've come to make life's most important commitment. No matter what they do for the rest of their lives, for one moment they've stood before God."

People strain for a close-up view of Graham through their binoculars. Bony young people recline in their wheelchairs and look on wistfully, their heads tilted in enchantment as he speaks of eternal joy. In some cities, the Chinese who don't speak English and others of foreign tongues listen through headphones to translations of Graham's sermons.

In a Graham sermon, he may sprinkle in a little social commentary—clucking at sensuous movie titles like *Voluptuous Vixens of '76* and song titles like *I Want to Do Something Freaky to You.*

He leavens his sermons with personal anecdotes, including one about his tearful schoolboy breakup with a Charlotte, North Carolina girl because she "wasn't Christian."

## Sermon Fundamentals

But all that is just filigree around the fundamentals of a Graham sermon:

THE SINNER'S SCENE-SETTER—"You're confused. You're empty. You're mixed up. . . . Many of you are suffering from religious or spiritual vertigo."

THE THREAT—"The time of your death has already been set. . . . Are you prepared to die? . . . There are thousands here tonight who are in the tomb of sin."

THE REMINDER OF POWERLESSNESS WITHOUT GOD—"You yourself do not have assurance and certainty. . . . You need forgiveness, hope, assurance, confidence."

THE URGENT ENTREATY—"This may be the most important hour you have ever spent. This hour may be the hour for which you were born. The decision you make tonight will decide for many of you your marriage, your vocation, your

WIDE WORLD

Examining a rack of nudist and men's magazines in a New York bookstore.

eternal destiny. . . . Think about it. . . . Just talk to the Lord like you would your best friend."

THE PROMISE—"You can come to Christ tonight and have your whole world turned around. . . . All you have to do is say, 'Jesus, have mercy upon me'. . . . He can heal the wounds of your soul tonight. . . . The lowly, miserable, low-down alcoholic, you come."

THE GUIDE—"This," he says, holding up a Bible in his palm like a waiter proudly hoisting his chef's finest souffle, "is the compass."

These are the fundamentals of Billy Graham's mission: sixty-six books of authority; sin, hell, and how to avoid it; faith, submission to Christ, salvation. "How many have your Bibles?" he normally asks his crusade audiences. "Lift them up. Thousands of Bibles!"

"The Bible says" is a common Graham sentence-opener, but he puts more emphasis on its general authority than on the literal meaning of its phrases. He doesn't dwell on theological controversies, like the continuing debate over biblical literalism. As Graham associate Grady Wilson advises Christians, "Don't go around spreading your doubts. They have enough of their own."

Graham says much Bible language is "symbolic." For example, when the beggar Lazarus died and the Gospel of St. Luke says he was carried by angels into Abraham's bosom, "that doesn't mean he climbed into his chest cavity," Graham says. "That means he went to where Abraham was. He went to heaven or paradise."

Graham believes there was an Adam and an Eve, that there was a Noah's Ark, and that a big fish swallowed Jonah and vomited him in the direction of dry land after three days.

Back in the 1940s, Graham also decided heaven was probably 1,600 miles long and 1,600 miles wide. "I dismissed that long ago," he says now, laughing at his attempt to visualize heaven. The Book of Revelation's portrait of a heaven of gold with gates of pearl is probably just symbolic language to entice people with a "fantastic" haven for the saved, he says.

He thinks Jesus may be spotted in heaven because He may still have the crucifixion scars in His hands, feet and side. But Graham says that's just speculation. "We know that Jesus had a different kind of a body after the resurrection," he says. "He could walk through closed doors."

The late Edward J. Carnell, a leading conservative theologian, wrote that Graham "preaches Christ in such clear and forceful language that even a bartender can find his way to the mercy seat. . . . The common man is weary of theories. He is hungry for the gospel. He craves a firm note of authority."

Others find Graham's authoritative style intimidating.

Dr. Wayne Oates, a Southern Baptist minister and professor of psychiatry at the University of Louisville in Kentucky, says many people who walk the aisle in a Graham crusade are "grasping at the straws of authoritarian reassurance at the mass level."

The greatest need of these people, says Oates, is for "one-to-one, careful attention over a longer period of time by a religious person who does not depend on authoritarian pronouncements but upon a faithful relationship of truth."

Graham defends himself by saying the Bible is authoritative about sin, too. And he says he doesn't leave his listeners in despair. "I ask them to come and receive Christ, and Christ takes away the sense of guilt and Christ gives them a sense of forgiveness. When we were in London, the head of a mental hospital said, 'If I could assure my patients that they were forgiven, I could release half of them because guilt is something that plagues the entire human race.'"

Billy Graham may make people squirm in their seats

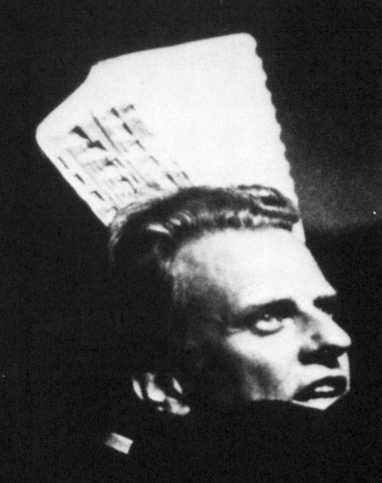

Former President and Mrs. Dwight D. Eisenhower with Mr. Graham and Dr. Edward L. R. Elson, pastor of the National Presbyterian Church, Washington, D.C.

about fooling around on their spouses, being homosexual, listening to sensual music, smoking, gambling or guzzling booze. But you don't often hear anything from Graham that would make white-collar criminals, slum landlords, manufacturers of armaments or crooked politicians wriggle uncomfortably.

Dr. J. Randolph Taylor, pastor of the twenty-five-hundred-member Myers Park Presbyterian Church in Charlotte, North Carolina, says Graham talks too much about the resurrected Jesus and not enough about "the bloody, sweaty Jesus," the outspoken revolutionary who shamed the world for its crimes against the poor and the outcast.

"Graham has had a diversionary influence on American Christianity," says Taylor, who grew up on the same Chinese mission field as Graham's wife Ruth, and whose father married the Grahams.

Graham contends that liberals like Taylor have overlooked some of his actions and sermons on social ethics. He reportedly insisted, against racist tradition, that blacks be allowed to sit anywhere at his 1953 crusade in Chattanooga, Tennessee.

His aides say he turned down invitations to hold a crusade in South Africa for twenty-two years, until 1973, when he was assured it could be racially integrated without interference from supporters of apartheid.

He has made several statements supporting organized labor, saying that if Jesus were alive today, he'd belong to a carpenters' union.

Graham's colleagues say he made stronger statements on political ethics to Presidents Eisenhower, Kennedy, Johnson and Nixon than were made public. But Graham didn't harangue them openly about the war in Vietnam and has never openly lobbied for broad social change.

Graham thinks morals are best improved by helping individuals to a spiritual rebirth. Collectively, born-again Christians can make the world more decent, he contends.

Billy Graham is basically a fatalist, however.

"In the real world in which we live," he says, "in which man is dominated by sin, he's going to fight and Jesus said there would be wars and rumors of war 'til the end of time. We're not going to legislate war out of existence. We're not going to legislate hate out of existence."

Several years ago, the Rev. J. Metz Rollins, Jr., then executive director of the National Committee of Black Churchmen, told a meeting of the group that Graham was "one of the most dangerous forces in this country." His statement was picked up by the news wires and he got some feisty letters from Graham followers.

But Rollins, now pastor of St. Augustine United Presbyterian Church in Bronx, New York, still maintains that Graham's "individualistic gospel" epitomizes the Protestant establishment that oppresses minorities. "Billy Graham is sort of a homogenized version of all the ills and extremes of American Christianity," says Rollins. "The church should speak out and raise the question of judgment. He does not speak the uncomfortable word. While he did fill Madison Square Garden, he did not touch the question of what it's like to live in a city like New York. Here in the Bronx, I see Con Edison cutting off the lights of folks, people wrestling with all the indifferences of welfare."

Harvey Cox, a theologian at Harvard Divinity School, is disappointed with Graham. "He was a man who had an enormous potential for bringing . . . a prophetic word to American society. He was like a young Amos coming out of the wild and ending up being the court theologian of one of the kings. That's not what we need in this country—domesticated prophets."

Billy Graham generally doesn't answer his critics. But his friend Grady Wilson sometimes answers them for him.

Wilson told a group of church people in Seattle in 1976: "We had clergymen in New York City who refused to have anything to do with the Billy Graham crusade. You know why? They said they didn't believe in emotionalism. But they did. A few months later Mr. Graham and I were watching them on the news one evening. They were in that civil rights march between Selma and Montgomery, Alabama, tears running down their cheeks, waving their hats in the air, shouting, screaming, laughing, crying and all the rest. They believe in emotionalism, but not when it comes to trying to win people to Jesus Christ."

Dr. Carl F. H. Henry of Arlington, Virginia, one of the country's most respected conservative theologians, offers a more temperate defense of Billy Graham. He says Graham's full influence on Christianity can't be measured until more of Graham's converts have had a chance to get into Christian work.

"One thing about Graham," says Henry, "he certainly broke into the mainstream of ecumenically oriented denominations with a personal gospel that, on the official level, had been pretty well put aside."

Graham says he has no idea how many people have been "saved" through his crusades. "You won't get accurate statistics until we get to heaven," he says.

Who will inherit Graham's mantle?

People often speculate that the Rev. Leighton Ford of Charlotte, husband of Graham's sister Jean, is the heir-apparent. He is vice-president and an associate evangelist of the Billy Graham Evangelistic Association.

Ford, in his mid-forties, says he and Graham have long had an understanding that he would take over Graham's work if the veteran evangelist died suddenly. Graham also says Cliff Barrows, in his fifties, his music, radio and television director, would be among the association's top leaders after his death.

And the Graham organization is working systematically to recruit top young evangelists to keep the group going in the future. The organization keeps files on a thousand young evangelists, some of whom will be asked to join the team someday, according to Graham.

"We have about three generations down the line, and some of them don't even know that they're the ones we will be asking 'cause it might hurt them at this moment," he said.

However, even Leighton and Jean Ford say they don't believe any evangelist will ever attain Graham's stature. "He's been given a unique role by the Lord and I don't think anybody else can fill that," says Ford. Jean Ford adds, "It will be very, very hard to shift loyalties from one dynamic personality to another."

Billy Graham, on the other hand, has a more modest response to questions about the future of his organization. "I could drop out right now," he says, "and I don't think it would miss a cog."

# 5.

# The Billy Graham Evangelistic Association

**B**illy Graham's ministry has grown so big financially that he says the large sums it earns sometimes are embarrassing. His groups need every penny of it and more, he says, but he worries that they seem too wealthy.

He's learned a lot of lessons about money.

Graham was accepting "love offerings"—special collections for his livelihood—from crusades until 1950. That year, the *Atlanta Constitution* ran two pictures—one of a beaming Graham as he left the city after a crusade and the other of grinning ushers holding big money bags. It looked like Graham was laughing all the way to the bank.

"It broke Billy's heart," says a close friend of Graham's. "He went to his knees in tears." The evangelist took the advice of a friend at the National Council of Churches and went on straight salary, now $39,500 a year.

The years have blessed the Graham ministry with

gifts of $25 million a year and an operation as sophisticated as that of secular moneymakers, but Graham's old uneasiness about big money has resurfaced.

After the *Charlotte Observer* reported on June 26, 1977 that Graham's ministry included the little-known $22.9 million purse called the World Evangelism and Christian Education Fund, Graham received criticism from unexpected quarters.

No one that summer questioned the fund's legality. It seemed to be a normal endowment, with $19.3 million of blue chip stocks like IBM and AT&T and $3.6

**On his first mission to a Soviet Bloc country, Graham, wearing traditional Hungarian hat and sheepskin coat, samples goulash.**

million in prime, undeveloped mountain land in western North Carolina.

But some of Graham's friends chided him for not publicizing the fund, so that all of his two million contributors would have full knowledge of it. As it was, although Graham had briefly mentioned the fund in interviews in the early 1970s, few of his donors, whose gifts of $8 to $10 provide ninety per cent of Graham's contributions, knew about it or how wealthy it was. Nor did at least one of his big donors.

J. Marse Grant, an old friend of Graham who used to play baseball against him in high school and now is editor of the *Biblical Recorder*, the weekly Southern Baptist publication for North Carolina, scolded Graham in a summer editorial, saying financial accountability is a "must" in mass evangelism.

Then R. G. Puckett, editor of the *Maryland Baptist*, that state's publication of the Southern Baptist Convention, Graham's own denomination, called the fund a case of "poor judgment." He wrote, "We take a dim view of redirecting contributions of trusting persons who sent money to the Graham organization assuming it would be used in direct and immediate evangelism."

World Evangelism has given money to conservative Christian groups, such as the weekly magazine *Christianity Today*, the Fellowship of Christian Athletes and Campus Crusade for Christ. It also has pledged to underwrite the costs of a new $14.5 million religious studies center, including a Billy Graham library, at the evangelist's alma mater, Wheaton College, and to build a Bible institute near Asheville, North Carolina.

Graham says World Evangelism was not a secret fund because its Form 990s—public tax returns required of most nonprofit groups—had been on file with the Internal Revenue Service since the fund was started. However, unless an inquirer to the IRS knows the name of an organization, he or she is unable to have the returns located in the agency's massive files.

In World Evangelism's case, it was begun as the Billy Graham Benevolent Fund early in 1970, became the Billy Graham Foundation later that year, the Billy Graham Evangelistic Trust in 1971 and, finally, World Evangelism in 1975.

Billy Graham has acknowledged that World Evangelism deliberately was not publicized. He says such lack of disclosure jibes with Matthew 6, where Jesus is recorded as having said, "But when thou doest alms, let not thy left hand know what thy right hand doeth: That thine alms may be in secret: and thy Father which seeth in secret himself shall reward thee openly."

"For another thing," Graham said in a statement on World Evangelism, "extensive publicity, we knew, would mean we would be inundated with requests for help which we could not begin to meet."

The Billy Graham Evangelistic Association (BGEA), the main arm of Graham's ministry, is on the Council of Better Business Bureau's list of charitable groups that do not meet its standards for full, audited financial information. The BGEA hasn't been required to give anybody, not even the government, financial data because the IRS considers it a church. While most tax-exempt groups, including World Evangelism and many other religious organizations, must file public financial reports with the IRS, churches do not.

George Wilson says that BGEA is not a church as such, but because the group asked for that status in 1953 and got it, it has not been questioned.

But in 1976, Billy Graham and his associates gave the *Charlotte Observer* skeletal financial figures on his ministry that provided one of the best glimpses of his money matters yet to appear in the news media, although the materials did not include information about World Evangelism.

Graham's unaudited summaries of expenditures for 1974 and 1975 showed that the Billy Graham Evangelistic Association, the main arm of his ministry, and

**Walking with the young through a village in western Nigeria.**

other Graham organizations have annual budgets totaling $40 million.

The evangelist's media reach is wide. Three or four of his crusades are televised each year and reach a potential ninety per cent of the viewing audience. His weekly radio program *Hour of Decision* is carried on about nine hundred stations around the world. His monthly *Decision* magazine has a circulation of nearly four million. His World Wide Pictures in Burbank, California, has produced about one hundred films, including *The Hiding Place,* seen by at least four million people. And the Billy Graham Evangelistic Association sends out one hundred million pieces of mail a year.

The Graham ministry's media saturation is "no different than what General Mills does with Wheaties," says George Wilson.

Each weekday morning at ten o'clock, Wilson receives a computer report telling how many gifts the ministry received the day before and their average size. He watches this report like a man watching the stock market and says, in fact, that the flow of donations, like the stock market, is a good economic indicator. "We feel an economic pinch sixty to ninety days before the stock market," says Wilson.

The Graham organization also includes two corporations in the book business. World Wide Publications, which publishes books, and the Grason Company, which sells them, do a total of about $1 million in business each year, according to Wilson.

In spite of its size, Billy Graham's operation does not look from the outside like the big time. Its Minneapolis headquarters, covering two city blocks in a rather seedy downtown area, is a lackluster, serious-business kind of place.

The Billy Graham people don't want to look rich. "You see, half of my work is abroad and all the [financial] information would be too big to them," Graham says. "By American standards it would be very small. I mean, a $20 or $25 million income is very small by American standards or church standards or Catholic standards but when you go to India and to Africa and all that and it's written up in the press it looks rather imposing and very affluent . . . They cannot possibly comprehend American standards."

Graham himself is financially comfortable although not nearly as rich as many people think.

In addition to his $39,500 salary, he has an undisclosed income from his syndicated column in 160 newspapers, royalties from his many books, $250,000 from the sale of land his father left him, and $290,000 worth of land he has acquired himself.

Graham says he's a millionaire only a few months each year—before he gives away income from his books. He says he has given royalties from his 1976 bestseller *Angels* to Wheaton College for its planned $14.5 million religious studies center and Graham library.

While some other evangelists ride around in Cadillacs, Billy Graham and his organization seem to prefer less ostentatious automobiles. The Grahams' taste runs more to Volvos and Jeeps.

Until the controversy over World Evangelism erupted, the closest Billy Graham had come to even a hint of financial indiscretion was during the Senate Watergate hearings. A White House memo surfaced that showed that the Nixon administration was willing to help Graham with IRS audits of his personal tax returns. But there was no indication Graham had sought such special favors and nothing ever came of the issue.

Graham says all his personal finances are handled by the trust department of the First Union National Bank in Charlotte. "For twenty-five years, I have never handled my personal affairs," he says. "I don't write checks, I don't pay bills. . . . Everything we own is in trust. We have nothing but the clothes on our backs."

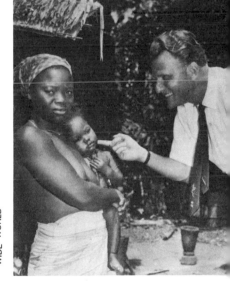

WIDE WORLD

**Evangelist Billy Graham tries to attract the attention of a Liberian child held in his mother's arms.**

# 6.

# Ambassador-at-large

When Richard Nixon was in the White House, says Billy Graham, the President sometimes would get Secretary of State Henry Kissinger and the evangelist together to talk about foreign affairs.

"Mr. Nixon always considered me somewhat of an authority on world affairs," Graham recalls. "He wanted to know what missionaries were thinking in certain countries because he felt that they knew more, many times, than the [American] embassy knew about what was going on because they were much closer to the people.

"I've had thirty years of traveling around the world, and I feel that I have some knowledge of world affairs and I've had the opportunity of talking to . . . a cross section in these countries that a lot of the traveling political leaders never see. . . .

"I meet the ambassadors, I meet the heads of state and I meet different people and talk to them and sometimes they'll tell me things they'll never tell a

(WORLD WIDE)

**On a tour of Africa, Billy rides a camel wearing an Arab headdress.**

visiting political leader—they'd never tell Kissinger, for example."

What catapulted Billy Graham, a North Carolina farmboy who never earned a graduate degree, into chats about world affairs with the likes of Nobel Peace Prize-winner Kissinger, Winston Churchill, Golda Meir and Queen Elizabeth?

Why would the president of Brazil, according to Grady Wilson, order a Graham crusade there to be shown on television during prime time? Why would the late Ethiopian emperor Haile Selassie close schools and open the royal stadium for a Graham rally?

In the past, it seems to have been good politics to be friendly with the world's best-known evangelist.

Graham and his wife relax on their porch in rocking chairs that Lyndon Johnson gave them because Graham had admired ones like them at Johnson's Texas home. Graham says he was even with Johnson for the late President's last night in the White House.

"... Johnson was the type of person that if I stayed in a hotel in Washington he'd say, 'What are you doing over there? Get over here, you know your room's here,'" Graham says. "He was a very generous man. ... He could love you and hug you or cuss you."

The evangelist, also a confidant of Presidents Eisenhower and Nixon and acquainted with Truman, Kennedy, Ford and Carter, calls it a "privilege" to view the presidency so closely.

But Graham vows he't not giving secular advice to political leaders anymore. "I don't think I would because of the CIA revelations . . . that they have used missionaries (to get foreign political information). . . . I would shy away now from giving counsel and advice to a President [that is] purely secular. Mine would be of a spiritual nature now. I had to learn that lesson the hard way."

Graham won't harp on "that lesson." But it's obvious his intimate relationship with Richard Nixon did little for Graham's generally pristine public image.

In 1976 Graham warned against bloc voting by Christians. "If a candidate gets in and falls on his face or corruption gets into his administration," he said, "then evangelical Christians are going to get blamed."

When it's hinted that politicians may consider his friendship a political liability because of his association with Nixon, Graham gets huffy. "You mean we've gone back to McCarthyism—guilt by association?" he asks. "That's what happened, really, to Nixon. They try to make everybody who ever knew him or shook his hand . . . somehow guilty and that's just not true. He had many marvelous people around him who were not in any way, shape or form connected with Watergate."

Charles Colson, special counsel and "hatchet man" to Richard Nixon and now a talk-showing, book-writing born-again Christian, says he doesn't think Nixon was "unmindful of the political benefits" of

(WIDE WORLD PHOTO)

(WIDE WORLD PHOTO)

being a friend of Billy Graham. And Colson says Nixon was "keenly interested in what Mr. Graham had to say about public opinion."

Nixon told his speechwriters to pay attention to the effective use of parables and repetition of statements in Graham sermons, according to William Safire, former Nixon speechwriter and now a columnist, in his 1975 book *Before the Fall*.

Charles Colson believes Graham has "taken a very bad rap" for his Nixon friendship and shouldn't be held accountable "for that particular President's moral failure."

Billy Graham still insists that he doesn't think Nixon took advantage of him. He tries to uphold Nixon's innocence on this point by recalling that Nixon called Graham during the 1960 presidential campaign and said, "Billy, your ministry is more important than my election, so you stay out of it."

Graham claims he has no records of his talks with Nixon and doesn't believe their conversations were

**Above right:** Billy Graham seated with Vice-President William R. Tolbert of Liberia greets tribal dancers who performed before him at Bigwaakor Village.

**Left:** Darwinian encounter: Billy Graham stares at a baboon and her offspring during his visit to Victoria Falls.

**Above left:** Members of a Hausa tribe watch as Mr. Graham washes his hands at a well in Lagos, Nigeria.

*The Man and His Ministry* 59

**"Johnson was the type of person that if I stayed in a hotel in Washington he'd say, 'What are you doing over there? Get over here. You know your room's here.' "**

taped by the former President because the two met in Nixon's private quarters. (Steve Stelzner, custodian of the Watergate files for the U.S. Senate Committee on Rules and Administration, says the index to the files shows no references to Graham but that indexing is not complete.)

". . . I made a deal with him [Nixon] that I would never keep notes after he became President . . . ," Graham said. "I told him, 'You want somebody you can talk to in confidence, that'll never quote you and never write memoirs about you.'"

Graham wasn't always so circumspect. In 1950, reporters caught him outside the White House after a visit with President Truman. The reporters talked the then thirty-one-year-old evangelist into kneeling on the White House lawn to recreate his prayer with the President.

Truman didn't like it, Graham recalls. "They asked all kinds of questions and I answered every one of them. I didn't know you're never supposed to quote the President."

Graham speaks about world politics with relish. It's obvious that he enjoys having red carpets rolled out for him in the world's palaces, and he'll tell stories by the hour about his experiences.

In January, 1968, he says, when Nixon was trying to decide whether to run for President, the evangelist was a guest at Nixon's Florida home. Graham had pneumonia in his right lung, but the two took walks, prayed, read the Bible and watched football together.

When Graham was leaving, he remembers the future President saying, "You still haven't told me what I ought to do [about running]." Graham turned and smiled and said, "Well, if you don't run, you'll always wonder."

Billy Graham still won't join in the chorus of Nixon denouncers, and he even hints that history may yet find a place of honor for Nixon.

"You travel to places like Israel where Golda Meir says he's the only President that ever kept his word all the way through and backed Israel to the hilt from start to finish. . . . I was in East Germany . . . with [U.S. Ambassador] John Sherman Cooper and he said, 'Over here . . . he [Nixon] is a very popular figure'. . . . We're too emotional over it [Watergate]. I sat at the tomb of Napoleon . . . in Paris and I remembered that he . . . died in disgrace. . . . Sixty years later they dug his bones up, brought him to Paris and gave him the greatest funeral in the history of Europe and the most magnificent tomb. . . . And I don't think any of us can quite figure out what history is going to do with all this."

Graham contends that Nixon had a "tremendous" sense of humor. Asked for examples of the Nixon wit, Graham recalled that Nixon would call Graham's rotund friend Grady Wilson "Greedy Grady" because Wilson made such good, long putts on the golf course. "He [Nixon] would say, 'How's Greedy Grady?' and

(WORLD WIDE)

**Billy shares a laugh with LBJ.**

then he would always pat Grady on the stomach and say, 'What about that tummy of yours? That's got to come down.'"

Wilson remembers when Nixon told him and Graham about his youthful conversion in California. "Having said that," said Wilson, "he gripped my arm and said, 'Pray for me, I'm a backslider.'"

When Nixon talked with Graham, said the evangelist, "Sometimes it would be political, sometimes it would be about this problem in Cambodia or Vietnam or something like that. I always tried to encourage him, as I have all Presidents, by quoting a verse of scripture or by saying, 'I'm praying for you that God will give you the right decision' and that sort of thing."

Graham says he believes the country would have been torn "wide apart" if Gerald Ford hadn't pardoned Nixon and if Nixon had been taken to court on the essential Watergate questions. And Graham feels sorry for Nixon. "Few men in American history," he says, "have ever suffered like he did."

Graham will unabashedly tell anecdotes which show his political naivete. For example, when Graham returned from a trip to India in 1956, he told President Eisenhower that the United States should give that nation an ultramodern white train as a symbol of peace. The scheme, which never came to pass, was born out of Graham's keen interest in public relations.

"Mr. Dulles [Secretary of State John Foster Dulles], while I was in India . . . had okayed a gift to them of $50 million. That was on the back pages of the [Indian] newspapers. On the same day the announcement came out, Mr. Bulganin [the late Soviet leader Nikolai Bulganin] and Mr. Krushchev had given Mr. Nehru [the late Indian Prime Minister] a white horse. Well, the white horse was on the front page of every paper in India. I said, 'The Indians don't know what $50 million means. They'll never see it. They'll never feel it, but they know what a horse is. Suppose they saw this

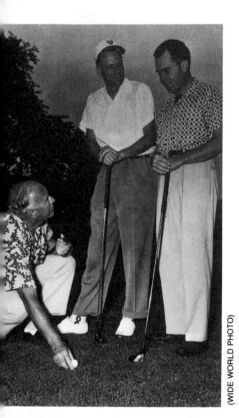

(WIDE WORLD PHOTO)

**Though he now feels that golf takes up too much time, Billy Graham is shown with then Vice-President Richard Nixon and Elmer Bobst, chairman of the board of a pharmaceutical concern.**

**Right: Former President Ford and Billy Graham on a golf course at Charlotte.**

white train going back and forth. . . .'"

But Dulles told Graham it wasn't a good idea.

Liberal religious leaders long have been exasperated at Graham's conservatism or fence-sitting on crucial human rights issues, especially his public silence on the Vietnam war. He admits now that he was against our prolonged "no-win" policy. And he adds, "If Americans ever go to war again, I think they ought to go to win."

To this day, he will not take a stand on whether the war was justified.

"If you lived back in the early 1960s, when Kennedy took over," he says, "it seemed to be [justified] because it seemed the Communists were going to take all of Southeast Asia and we had treaties with those people. . . . Up until 1967 almost everybody in America was for it. . . . The first time I ever heard of Vietnam was from President Kennedy and that was in a locker room before he became President and he was determined that we were going to stop the Communists from taking Southeast Asia."

Graham says he's "no pacifist, especially when it came to World War II." But he has never served in the military.

He was commissioned a lieutenant in the Army chaplaincy in 1944 but got the mumps while waiting to go to chaplain's school at Harvard. Then, while recovering, Graham wrote the chief of chaplains for a discharge to work for Youth for Christ, an international fundamentalist organization.

"I felt I could reach more servicemen and accomplish my ministry a great deal more than if I went into chaplaincy because so much of the chaplaincy is just routine desk work, which didn't appeal to me," Graham says.

On Northern Ireland and some other current issues, Graham says, "equally devout Christians may be on both sides." He says he is pro-integration and anti-apartheid, but he still hasn't taken a stand on other

(WIDE WORLD PHOTO)

**Then Vice-President Gerald Ford talks with Mr. Graham at the start of the pro-am at the Kemper Open at Charlotte, North Carolina.**

**Left: Graham with then Governor Jimmy Carter in Atlanta.**

(WORLD WIDE)

(WIDE WORLD PHOTO)

A royal welcome by King Hussein of Jordan at the Royal Basman Palace in Amman.

Below right: After this visit with Alexander Solzhenitsyn in a Stockholm hotel, Dr. Graham said the author's "grasp of both history and theology is amazing."'

Left: Chatting with then Prime Minister, Mrs. Indira Gandhi.

controversial issues.

He's against promiscuity, drugs for amusement, and pornography, but he still won't come down one way or the other on the death penalty, which he says he is still studying. But in typical Graham fashion, he has dropped a clue to his thinking on the subject, while not taking the clear kind of stand that could hold him up to criticism. After announcing he still hadn't decided about the death penalty, he said in the summer of 1977, "When you hear [about] a man like Son of Sam and people like that, it makes you wonder."

He often will become annoyed when reporters try to pin him down on current political topics. "There are more than twenty-five wars going on right now in the world. How would I be able to stand and say, 'God says you're right and you're wrong . . .?' It would be impossible and I'd be a fool."

Although Graham thinks people should work toward world peace and justice, he doesn't believe the world is going to be decent until Jesus returns.

But, he says, "The Bible teaches that as Christian believers we're to be the light of the world and the salt of the earth, which means we have tremendous re-

sponsibilities toward alleviating poverty and these things . . . but I don't see much possibility at the moment unless we have a moral and spiritual renaissance."

Graham says all problems are rooted in "spiritual" failure. "Our hearts are set on money, what kind of automobile I can get, how many food stamps I can get," he says. "I'm for giving people better housing, but that doesn't bring back the spirit. . . . I've noticed that many intellectuals are growing disillusioned today. They're disillusioned because the problem of the human is a spiritual problem."

Poverty exists, he says, because of social injustices, becauses churches have not met their responsibilities and because of overpopulation, food shortages, droughts, disease, and other natural disasters.

**Billy Graham addresses a Presidential Prayer Breakfast in 1963. Shown at far left is former President John F. Kennedy. At far right is former President Lyndon B. Johnson.**

President Nixon shakes the hand of Billy Graham as the President unveils a plaque honoring the evangelist.

WIDE WORLD

He injects a note of fatalism into his social philosophy. "Jesus said the poor ye shall have with ye always. There have always been the poor in every country. . . . There are poor in Russia today, there are poor in China today and there are the rich in Russia and there are the rich in China. Man has always been the same."

Graham foresees a world dictatorship, as predicted in the book of Revelation.

"One nation after another is coming under either a right-wing or a left-wing dictatorship," he says. "The Bible teaches there is coming a time when Antichrist is going to appear on the scene and he'll be a world dictator. He'll be on the scene for a very brief time. He'll be a man of peace. He'll bring peace to the world and prosperity to the world, and then he will turn on the Jew and the Christian and start his persecutions. Then will come the Battle of Armageddon with their nuclear weapons or whatever kind of weapons they'll have at that period of time."

Then, says Graham, "Christ is going to come back and set up His kingdom and we're going to have peace on earth and all the things we ever dreamed of. Poverty will be eliminated, injustice will be eliminated, and we're going to have a marvelous utopia on this planet with Christ as the ruler."

Adviser to the Mighty.

(WIDE WORLD PHOTO)

# 7.
# The Mystique

**W**hen a Seattle newspaper quoted a minister's sermon criticizing Billy Graham's theology in the spring of 1976, a widow fired off a letter to the lesser-known cleric suggesting that he "fade away."

"For your information," she advised him, "you couldn't begin to hold a candle . . . to Dr. Graham in any way—your speech, knowledge, stature, appearance, and in just any way you may think. There isn't a person in the whole world who gets the audience that he does and the world can't be wrong."

Queen Elizabeth came to the evangelist's defense once when a British chaplain asked Graham if conversions at his crusades "stick." According to a Graham aide, "As quick as a flash, Her Majesty spat out, 'Sir, of *course* they stick.' "

When a couple picketed against Graham's politics at his 1976 Seattle crusade, they might as well have been hanging Jesus in effigy. People heading into the crusade called them "jackasses" and "stupid." One meek young man protested to the demonstrators, "It's not in good taste. It's . . . it's . . . like desecrating a grave."

For many evangelical Christians, Billy Graham is hallowed ground, and stepping on him is like trampling the Bible.

This man Graham is a country boy from Mecklenburg County, North Carolina, and not renowned for any great intellect, any academic distinctions or any particularly novel ideas. But even apart from the super-slick organization that keeps him in the public eye, Billy Graham does possess a contagious faith in God and a compelling way of selling that faith to millions.

In a disillusioning world, he has been for many people the only untarnished hero left—maybe the one lasting example of clean living, self-discipline and good citizenship. He has been Uncle Sam with a Bible in his hand.

Graham, who says he's been asked to run for President, be a movie star and start a multimillion-dollar university, works hard to hold onto that esteem.

Some evangelicals see Graham as "their man in the world," says Dr. Robert W. Ross, a University of Minnesota religious scholar. "They think, 'This is the person who is saying what I would say if I had the gifts . . . because this is the message that everybody needs.' He represents an American tradition of the voice of God in the land of opposition to trends—sort of a religious fearlessness, sort of what you might call a heavenly honesty. He is America's religious world figure. To many, he is the ultimate American."

When people gather below Graham at his crusades to answer his call to give their lives to Christ, many of them stare at him, star-struck.

"Just like in Jesus' day . . . they came out of curiosity

(WIDE WORLD PHOTO)

**Though he admits that a career in films has been offered to him, perhaps the closest Billy Graham ever came was this meeting with Barbara Stanwyck, left and Betty Hutton, right during a visit to studios in Hollywood.**

or they came out of admiration or they came out of sincerity or they came out of [spiritual] hunger,'' says the Rev. T. W. Wilson, Graham's aide-de-camp. ''However, they come, I guess the important thing is that they come. There is the idea of hero worship. Billy Graham himself doesn't desire that.''

To maintain his respected image and good name, Billy Graham can't afford anything but a G-rated display of whimsy.

''I have to think of everything I say,'' he says, ''how it's going to look out of context and I also have to think of what the headline writer will write.''

**Holding his bible while gesturing with a jabbing forefinger Graham makes his points during a 10-day Southeastern Michigan Crusade at Pontiac Stadium.**

*The Man and His Ministry* 71

# 8.

# Following Romans 14:21

**G**raham says he and his aides operate by Romans 14:21—"It is good neither to eat flesh, nor to drink wine, nor any thing whereby thy brother stumbleth, or is offended, or is made weak." They apply that Christian principle in many ways.

Graham says he is never alone, even in a car, with a secretary or any woman other than his wife or a female relative because "the Bible says to avoid the appearance of evil." And he doesn't want to be framed by a woman claiming the world's leading evangelist made sexual advances at her.

"I keep myself pretty well surrounded [by staff, family or friends], so they would have a pretty hard time," Graham says with a laugh. "I've heard of people who've been found in somebody's room and they take a picture real quick. I've never had that, but I don't rule out that somebody may try to frame me at some point."

Years ago, he says, an older evangelist told him,

"You're young and virile and women are almost always attracted to evangelists and pastors."

He will not see a woman journalist alone at his home, and when he sees one at his office down the mountain, he leaves his door open, with secretaries clacking away at typewriters nearby.

Billy Graham says he'd rather be killed than commit adultery, but he doesn't mind at all talking about his brushes with sexual peril. The closest he's come to a risque public scene, he says, was in London's Soho district:

"This girl . . . was handed over the other people. I saw her coming and I said, 'Good night and God bless you,' and I jumped in the middle of some policemen. She was on drugs and . . . she was going to undress and have her picture taken because all the television cameras were there. She finally was able to get on top of our car, and as we left they had a picture of her on top of the car and it was on the front page of every newspaper in Britain."

Graham winces at being photographed with anything looking like liquor in his hand. At a reception in Liberia several years ago, a glass of champagne was slipped into his hand just as pictures were being snapped. "I don't know that it ever appeared in the newspaper," he says, "but I thought about it anyway."

Graham says he believes the Bible teaches moderation in drinking, but not total abstinence. He thinks the teetotaling notion that Jesus turned water into grape juice, not wine, is "ridiculous."

"On moral or religious grounds, I wouldn't hesitate to take a sip of wine, but I don't," he says. "I have tasted wine, especially in Europe where it's not offensive, but, no, I'm not a drinker. Even people who drink would be disappointed, maybe, because I remember a certain clergyman who was the chaplain of one of our major political parties. Many years ago he went to Honolulu and drank with the rest of them and tried to be buddy-buddy with everybody and some of the people came back and they were drinkers themselves but they didn't have respect for him drinking."

After Graham was quoted in the *Miami Herald* in late 1976 on his drinking views—fairly moderate by Bible Belt standards—he came down harder against alcoholic beverages. "It is my judgment that because of the devastating problem that alcohol has become in America, it is better for Christians to be teetotalers except for medicinal purposes," he said, to answer criticism from temperance types. Graham also says his wife had followed a doctor's advice several years ago and taken a glass of port wine each night for an "allergy."

The evangelist says that if he had ever left preaching, he could have been:

A presidential candidate. Leading politicians in both major parties have asked him to run, he says. "They just try every day, every way, to get him in politics," says his right-hand man T. W. Wilson.

The holder of "top positions," including ambassadorships, in presidential administrations, according to his aides. Details on those offers won't come out until "somebody's memoirs," Graham says.

A U.S. senator. During the 1950s, Graham says, some North Carolina Democratic leaders asked him to fill the unexpired term of a deceased senator.

A movie star. The late film producer Cecil B. De Mille wanted Graham to star in his biblical movies, the evangelist says.

A university president. Graham says a man he won't identify offered him $10 million and 1,000 acres to start a university, but Graham refused.

Since 1955, Graham has shown up more frequently

(WIDE WORLD PHOTO)

**Making a beeline for the clubhouse Arnold Palmer shares a laugh with Billy Graham.**

among the Gallup Poll's ten men most admired by Americans than any other man. The poll hasn't been taken since 1974, but Graham made his best showing in the last five years of the survey—second to Richard Nixon from 1969 to 1972 and to Henry Kissinger in 1973 and 1974.

Billy Graham has received dozens of honorary doctorates and is called "Dr. Graham" by aides talking about him to reporters and other outsiders, even though the evangelist has no earned doctorate.

As further evidence of his stature, Graham was 1971 grand marshal of the Tournament of Roses Parade, the first clergyman so honored. Other grand marshals have been such all-American pop figures as Walt Disney, Bob Hope, the Apollo 12 astronauts and Roy Rogers and Dale Evans.

That Tournament of Roses appearance was the pinnacle of Billy Graham's role as "the endorser of America," says Martin Marty, professor of modern church history at the University of Chicago Divinity School and associate editor of *Christian Century* magazine.

Graham's friends often tell stories that portray him and his colleagues more as a bunch of endearing rubes than the globe-trotting celebrities that they are.

For instance, there's the one about how Graham wanted to applaud a city's low rate of traffic fatalities. Instead, the story goes, he said it had been about a year since they'd had a fertility.

One of the most-told Graham yuks is about the time in 1965 when aide T. W. (pronouned Tee-Dubyah) Wilson was driving his boss from Atlanta to Graham's home in Montreat, North Carolina, in a rain storm. Graham, sick and feverish after a crusade in Honolulu, was snoozing in the back seat.

While Wilson was inside a Georgia truck stop getting directions, Billy went into a bathroom. Wilson drove off, thinking Billy was still napping in the back.

A sleepy, rumpled Graham waited for his pal and then finally took a cab to Greenville, South Carolina. Because the evangelist was in his shirtsleeves in the rain and prodding the driver to catch up with Wilson's car, the driver suspected he was transporting an escaped convict or some other kind of culprit, as Wilson tells it.

It wasn't until a Greenville Holiday Inn operator greeted Graham with a hug and a "Hey, Billy!" that the driver was convinced it indeed was Billy Graham.

T. W. Wilson says that's the only Billy Graham story to ever make the front page of the Russian daily newspaper *Pravda*.

Not all the Graham foul-ups are funny. In fact, some of them have been downright devastating to his standing.

Perhaps his most monumental gaffe was in South Africa in 1973, when he said that rapists should be castrated. Many people were aghast and called the comment "barbaric," but Graham pulled out of the goof with typical ease.

Twelve days after making the statement, he released another saying it had been "an offhand, hasty, spontaneous remark at a news conference that I regretted as soon as I said it." While assuaging some of the outrage, Graham also probably stroked his law-and-order supporters with the added comment that some people reacted more violently to the idea of castration than to rape itself and that that response was "a part of our permissive society's sickness."

Billy Graham's Christian acquaintances form a network of evangelicals around the world. They range in background from Walter Hoving, chairman of Tiffany's in New York, to Black Panthers founder and newly "born again" Christian Eldridge Cleaver.

Many people who claim they were led to Christ through Billy Graham's message say the evangelist helped turn them from a life of agnosticism or drunkenness to one of a humble, well-behaved Christian.

The account of Dr. David Maclagan is a good example of the good-versus-evil struggle these Graham convertees say was fought out within them when they heard Billy Graham preach. Maclagan says he was the agnostic son of a minister until he heard Graham in England in the 1950s.

Dr. Maclagan, then a stranger to Graham and a student at Cambridge University, recalls a spiritual force that spoke to him in a crowd of thousands. Maclagan says he was "very, very anti the church" then and opposed an American evangelist chastising the British about their sins, as Graham was doing.

A curious Maclagan, who was determined to figure out Graham's mystique, decided that people were drawn to the evangelist because of his personality and handsomeness, the drama of his crusades, the "tear-jerker" hymns sung by crusade singer George Beverly Shea, plus the general gullibility of most people.

But Graham started "getting to" Maclagan, he says, when the evangelist spoke to students at a university church. Neither Shea nor a choir was there. The fact that conversions were heavy among an overflow crowd in a nearby church, where worshippers could hear but not see Graham, hurt Maclagan's theory, he says.

"He started off by saying that he was under no illusion—that before him was one of the most intellectual audiences that could be assembled anywhere in Britain at one time and because of that he was not going to argue or debate with us on matters of personal belief," Maclagan says.

"He said he wasn't overly concerned about what we thought about the Bible. The question he was going to put before us was what did we think of Jesus Christ. He immediately came on my wavelength. I had always been an admirer of the ethic and the teaching of Jesus Christ, even though I had turned off from the institutionized church."

But Maclagan didn't succumb to Graham's preaching that night. "I wasn't as easy as that," he says.

"But I couldn't get Billy Graham out of my mind," and he returned to the crusade. Maclagan's description of what happened sounds like Graham's own conversion through a fiery, sinner-pointing pulpiteer in 1934. In Graham's case, the evangelist had announced "There's a great sinner in this place tonight," and Graham, then sixteen, thought the preacher was talking about him.

Maclagan also thought Graham was speaking directly to him. It happened after Graham had made his altar call and people had gathered in front. Maclagan stayed in back of the arena.

"To my utter amazement," he recalls, "he [Graham] said he had a strong feeling that there was a young man somewhere in this audience that was struggling to get up the courage to come forward. He hadn't even finished before I was out of my seat."

Maclagan says he got lost on his way to the front. "I was walking along this vast corridor and passed this exit and the doors suddenly burst open. This beautifully dressed man met me . . . [and] said, 'This is the young man I've come for.'"

The man, a teacher and crusade counselor, wasn't scheduled to be at the crusade that night, according to Maclagan, who says the man had been grading papers at home when he got a "feeling" he should go to the crusade.

"Nobody to this day can convince me it was a coincidence," says Maclagan, who was counseled by the man that night and converted. Maclagan now is a minister of the Church of Scotland.

Billy Graham has a number of other spiritual trophies—people who say Graham's savior-like influence retrieved them from a low spiritual period.

Graham's Los Angeles crusade in 1949 saved their lives, say two highly visible "sinners" of that time.

Jim Vaus, a wiretapper for the big gambling kingpin Michey Cohen, said if he hadn't made a spiritual about-face that night in Los Angeles and changed his schedule, Federal Bureau of Investigation agents told him he probably would have been killed in an ambush planned by a rival crime syndicate. Vaus now says he's a Presbyterian who heads a youth counseling service in San Diego.

Louis Zamperini, an Olympic track star and World War II hero-turned-alcoholic, thinks he would have drunk himself to death if he hadn't heard Graham preach in Los Angeles. Zamperini now teaches skiing and mountain climbing to delinquent boys in California.

Even Oral Roberts, generally considered America's second most important evangelist, was once bitter about Billy Graham's good-gut image but now says he "would do anything for Billy."

In the 1950s, Graham was enjoying a favorable press when Roberts' healing ministry was being called fakery. When the two evangelists crossed paths in New York and Graham invited Roberts to visit him, Roberts refused. "I was hurt that he was being given a clean bill of health," Roberts says now.

Instead, according to Roberts, Graham visited him. "I said, 'Billy, they're praising you to the sky and knocking me, and it hurts,'" Roberts relates. "And then he did the greatest thing. He put his hands on my shoulders and he said, 'I would do anything in the world if God had given me the gift of helping sick people that He's given you.' That experience marked my life—that the No. 1 evangelist in the world would come to my room and offer me encouragement."

But how will religious historians view Billy Graham a hundred years from now?

Harvey Cox, a theologian at Harvard Divinity School, says a centry from now Graham's historical significance may be "as one of the major people to make use of the mass media and mass marketing techniques in religion."

Martin Marty, long a tough critic of American Christianity as an associate editor of the liberal *Christian Century* magazine, says that Graham, to his credit, avoided picking up the "mean, radical right" fundamentalism of the 1920s. Instead, said Marty, Billy Graham "slicked up the manners of the old fundamentalists."

Marty says that Graham has kept alive the dream of a Christian America—"The dream of everybody from Columbus, the Puritans, the Virginians, everybody except the Jews as far as large groups go."

In the 1950s, Marty says, the cold war was at its peak and Americans were worried about their nation's direction, but Graham stepped forward to tell the nation it wasn't beyond hope.

Graham was eclipsed by other religion newsmakers in the 1960s, such as Vatican II and Martin Luther King, Jr. "American religion is plagued by innings and the sixties wasn't Graham's inning," Marty says, adding that Graham may make a comeback in the 1970s because of the decade's revivial of individualistic religion.

While Graham seems to be constantly standing in judgment on America, "more than any other individual, he has convinced America that fundamentally we are on the right track," says Marty. "He very much endorses the world as we like it. A hundred years from now, people will look back and say 'Billy Graham made America feel good.'

"He's a page out of our old family album."

(WIDE WORLD PHOTO)

**Mrs. Anne Morrow Graham sits with her son at Madison Square Garden during a crusade.**

# Appendices

## Graham's Views

*On whether he was embarrassed by his wife's taking a sign from a demonstrator at a 1975 celebration of Mecklenburg County's bicentennial:*

"No [Graham laughs] . . . On one side I wished she'd left it to the police and on the other side I was sort of proud of her. We found out, of course, that she was legally within her rights due to the fact that she had come to hear the President [Ford]. A man [Dan Pollock of Charlotte] had come and stood in front of her and [held] the sign ["Eat The Rich"] in front of her where she couldn't see the President of the United States and this was interfering with her rights. I suspect that she would do it again."

(Pollock filed assault charges against Mrs. Graham, but the case was dismissed. "I wasn't blocking her view," Pollock said recently. "She was on the front row. . . . I was in the aisle at about the third row. She walked back to me.")

*On why he's a member of the First Baptist Church in Dallas rather than a church near his Montreat home:*

"I joined [the Dallas church], I suppose, twenty-five years ago and to break after twenty-five years would be a very difficult thing. When they change pastors I might change but even that's problematical. I have so many friends in the church. There's no Baptist church in Montreat . . . and then if I belonged to a local church they would expect me to be at every little meeting that they had."

*On political systems:*

"I think the free enterprise system, which I'd rather call it than capitalism, is the best device that man has,

but I don't think it's the only one that Christians can support. We are a socialist society compared to, let's say, the days of Franklin Roosevelt. There has to be a certain amount of socialism.''

*On the ordination of women:*
''I don't object to it like some [Christians] do because so many of the leaders of the early church were women. They prophesied, they taught. You go on the mission fields today and many of our missionaries are women who are preachers and teachers.''

*On women as church pastors:*
''I think it's coming, probably, and I think it will be accepted more and more. I know a lot of women who are far superior to men when it comes to ministering to others. . . . Who would say that Corrie Ten Boom (a Dutch Christian who helped Jews escape the Nazis during World War II and now tells her story around the world) is not ordained of God to preach? They [such women] are ordained of God whether they had men to lay hands on them and give them a piece of paper or not. I think God called them.''

*On the nation's race relations:*
''I see very little possibility of the North solving its racial problems. The blacks and the whites do not know each other. In the South they know each other. They are friends. When the servant-master relationship is finished in the next generation I think the South will have pretty well solved its racial problem and it's headed that way very fast right now. I think Mr. Carter's emergence is indicative of that, with the black support of a peanut farmer from Georgia.''

# Graham's Favorite Verses

When asked for his favorite Bible verses, Graham said the following Bible passages ''meant a great deal to me in my Christian experience'' and explained why.

(WORLD WIDE)

(WIDE WORLD PHOTOS)

*I Corinthians 10:13*

There hath no temptation taken you but such as is common to man: but God is faithful, who will not suffer you to be tempted above that ye are able; but will with the temptation also make a way to escape, that ye may be able to bear it.

"Often when I have faced trial and temptation, I have quoted this verse to myself, and it has been a great encouragement and comfort to me. It indicates that when temptation comes, God always provides a way to escape. The Scriptures indicate that we are tempted daily, thus a verse like this memorized can be a great comfort and strength to the Christian."

*Luke 12:15*

And he said unto them, Take heed, and beware of covetousness: for a man's life consisteth not in the abundance of the things which he possesseth.

"This would indicate that our lives are far more than materialism. This is why so many people in the affluent western world are disillusioned. Our postwar obsession with materialistic things has brought about a great sense of emptiness and boredom. I often quote this verse and similar ones to myself so that I do not get absorbed with the materialism of our age. There are other deeper spiritual and moral things that are much more important to building character and preparing one for eternity."

*Proverbs 3:11*

My son, despise not the chastening of the Lord; neither be weary of his correction.

"It has been my experience that when I get off track, God has a way of spanking me and putting me back on the straight and narrow. He has had to chastise me many times in my life. Many times His discipline has 'hurt,' but it has been good for me. I know He has always done it from a heart of love."

*Proverbs 3:5–6*

Trust in the Lord with all thine heart; and lean not unto thine own understanding. In all thy ways acknowledge Him, and He shall direct thy paths.

"This was the second passage my mother taught me when I was a child. I suppose I have quoted it more than any other passage, except John 3:16."

*Philippians 4:13*

I can do all things through Christ which strengthenth me.

"I have quoted this passage when a challenge was too great, or I became bone weary in the midst of a long crusade, or I became discouraged. Concerning the great prophet Elijah, the Scripture says he was 'a man of like passions.' So am I. I need the encouragement of God's word daily."

*John 3:16*

For God so loved the world, that He gave His only begotten Son, that whosoever believeth in Him should not perish but have everlasting life.

"These twenty-five words actually compose the entire Gospel. John 3:16 is a Bible in miniature. It is the very essence and heart of what I believe and preach."

*Matthew 25:35–36*

For I was an hungred, and ye gave me meat: I was thirsty, and ye gave me drink: I was a stranger, and ye took me in: Naked, and ye clothed me: I was sick, and ye visited me: I was in prison, and ye came unto me.

"I believe that I once gave to Sargent Shriver 200 passages of Scripture that deal with our responsibility to the poor, when he was head of the poverty program (U.S. Office of Economic Opportunity). He and I made a motion picture together on our responsibility of helping the poor."